Stories of Courage, Success and Hope

GROWING UP BLACK

As told by ALISON HAMMOND, KYE WHITE, LOLLY ADEFOPE, KWAJO TWENEBOA, EUNICE OLUMIDE, PATRICE LAWRENCE and PAUL CANOVILLE

IN BRITAIN

STUART LAWRENCE

SCHOLASTIC

To my son, Theo, my wife, Angela, my mum, my dad, my sister, my nephew, Ethan, my niece, Mia, and all my wider family. Thank you for continuing to support me, lift me up, and show me that I can do anything I set my mind to. I'd also like to dedicate this book to all the young people out there who might doubt the possibilities of where they can reach – always aim to get to the highest point and to be the best that YOU can be.

"Aim for the moon. If you miss, you may hit a star."
– W. Clement Stone

Scholastic will donate 25p per copy sold to The Prince's Trust to help transform young lives. The Prince's Trust is incorporated by Royal Charter in England: RC000772. Registered charity number in England and Wales: 1079675 and Scotland: SC041198

Published in the UK by Scholastic, 2023
1 London Bridge, London, SE1 9BG
Scholastic Ireland, 89E Lagan Road, Dublin Industrial Estate, Glasnevin, Dublin, D11 HP5F

Text © Stuart Lawrence, 2023
Contributor interviews written up by Ashley Hickson-Lovence
Cover illustration by Simone Douglas
Inside photograph, p149 © Simon Frederick, 2021

ISBN 978 07023 1585 5

A CIP catalogue record for this book is available from the British Library.

Printed in China
Paper made from wood grown in sustainable forests and other controlled sources.

3 5 7 9 10 8 6 4 2

www.scholastic.co.uk

CONTENTS

Stuart Lawrence

GROWING UP BLACK IN BRITAIN

Growing up in Britain, London to be specific, was completely normal to me as I had nothing else to compare it to, but as I've grown older, I've realized that my London experience has actually been quite unusual. This is because of the huge amount of diversity on every street and in every home around me. With all these different people in such a relatively small area compared to the rest of Britain, there are not many options other than to find ways of getting on and making it work. I have been interviewing some amazing people from around the country, and the stories I have heard have ranged from happy to sad and everything in between. Once I had listened and processed it all, I thought it was only fitting to sit down and write about my own experience of growing up Black in Britain.

The main area where I spent most of my childhood was a place called Woolwich, in southeast London. My life spent around a council estate was just magical. Even though the estate was mostly made up of flats and maisonettes, we were among the lucky ones with an entire house to ourselves. A house with a garage and a garden seemed rather important to my mum and dad, who in the first years of their marriage had lived in a flat that hadn't come with either of those extras.

I went to the nursery and primary school nearest to our home. I had a great school life, although I wasn't the best academically. Still, I gave it a go and always tried my hardest. I found that I was better at creative and practical subjects such as art, and especially design tech, where I loved making things such as cakes and key rings. I enjoyed sport as well, and I loved being part of as many teams as I could.

Luckily for me, my secondary school was quite sporty, and was unusual as it actually had an indoor swimming pool on site, as well as a number of other sporting facilities. It was an all-boys school and was fairly diverse compared to others. I was one of two Black kids in my class, and there were also kids in my year of Chinese, Indian and Turkish heritage. No one was looked down on based on race – it was all about how intelligent you were, or how well you could play football! It felt right that people were judged on those aspects rather than their skin colour or how much money or stuff they had.

The defining moment of my childhood was obviously losing my older brother Stephen, who was murdered in an unprovoked attack when he was eighteen, but I had many unforgettable, funny and difficult moments separate to that. Before the loss of Stephen I honestly thought my life would be nothing major, pretty stable, and one that just plods along. That was me. That's what I thought I'd have to enjoy for the rest of my life before Stephen was murdered. That has turned out not to be the case, and I've been places, done things and met people that I could never have imagined back then in my wildest dreams, for which I am truly thankful. But it is all in honour of my brother. I try to ensure in all that I do that I keep his legacy and memory alive every day.

Stephen is probably the most recognized person in my family, but my Great Aunt Lillian, who is now one of the eldest members of our family, also has a significant story to tell. She was a local councillor in the borough of Lewisham as well as being a librarian, which was something that she was very proud of. Becoming a councillor was her way of ensuring that the views and opinions of the local people were heard. This was especially important to her as she was a mother of children that had dual heritage, which felt more unusual in those days. She was married to my Uncle Ed, who was a white man, and they had three kids together. I am sure when this happened that there must have been some people who had issues with their relationship, but for me, they are the example of a perfect, harmonious couple. They now live in Florida, USA, but my great aunt continues to work in education and makes herself an integral part of the local communities there, helping others where she can. As you might be able to tell, helping others is a massive part of who we are as a family, and is one of my core values.

Your sense of identity and other people knowing who you are and where you're from is so important to everyday life. We're constantly asked to declare who we are, ticking boxes on endless forms, putting ourselves in easy-to-understand categories, so that others can feel more comfortable about how and what they communicate with you and, in turn, how you might think of them. This is what first made me interested in writing this book. So here goes: I am Black English, but usually there is no opportunity for me to select that, so I tick "Black British".

My parents did what many people living in the Caribbean in the 20th century did. They believed that Britain wanted them and that there were opportunities for their children to have better lives here than they did in Jamaica.

My mum was sent for at the age of eleven or twelve to come and live with her mother and her new stepfather in England. She attended an English secondary school and one of her first jobs after leaving school was working at the bank as a cleaner. She had decided before Stephen died that she was going to go to university to become a schoolteacher.

My dad first came to the UK when he was eighteen and worked as an upholsterer for two years. He returned to Jamaica for a couple of years, then came back to London, where he continued as an upholsterer and eventually became a painter and decorator.

If you ever have the lucky experience of visiting Jamaica, you will know that it must have been one of the most complex decisions for my dad to choose to leave such a beautiful environment, one where he was part of the majority, to move to the UK and be in a minority. But he did it to ensure that his future kids would be able to benefit from the increased opportunities available here compared to the ones in Jamaica. (On reflection, I do sometimes wish that he had stayed in Jamaica, as I love it there so much!)

For me, cultural heritage is a bit like the sea; a living, breathing and free-flowing entity surrounding you and your family, showing where you are in the world at that moment in time and impacting how other people perceive you. It's about where you have come from, where you want to go, what you want the world to know about you and what has shaped you into the person you are today.

So for me, heritage is something that I feel deep in my bones and inside my heart. I remember hearing the phrase that we are "standing on the shoulders of giants" in terms of how far things have come and the work that's already been done. Someone wise once said to me that even though that is true, today we are guardians of the work that has been done so far because we are the bridge between the past and the future. We are charged with ensuring that tomorrow is a better place than the world today.

And that statement is the reason I feel so passionate about the work that I do, and why I try so hard each day, in the hope that I can make a difference for tomorrow. But that's enough about me. Read on to hear more from some incredible and generous people who have shared their experiences with me about growing up Black in Britain.

Kye
Whyte

IF SOMEONE TELLS ME I CAN'T DO SOMETHING, I HAVE TO PROVE THEM WRONG

Kye Whyte is a Black British BMX racer. He was a silver medallist at the 2020 Summer Olympics.

Growing up, BMX bikes were the new thing on the scene and a craze that had seemed to arrive from the USA. I remember my childhood and Christmases fondly, and one year was especially excellent: Santa Claus had brought me and my brother identical BMX bikes! The only difference was that one was marked with blue tape and the other with yellow tape. That silver BMX was my pride and joy, and even though it had snowed that Christmas, I tried to go out on it straight away.

It's pretty amazing how that bike, which I just saw as a passing phase, has now become part of the Olympics and our sporting culture. So, who better to talk to about his experiences of growing up Black in Britain than Olympian Kye Whyte?

I have a belief about families, that the youngest sibling usually learns from all the experiences of their elders in order to try and avoid the classic pitfalls. They take all the good bits and the bad bits, and put them together to become the most successful one out of a talented family. I believe that Kye truly backs up my thinking and is the epitome of that!

A childhood of trying to keep a young mind focused and out of trouble has created this incredible young man, an Olympic silver medallist and European champion. Kye is a typical example of what is needed to become one of the greats in this world, with his steely focus and his determination to prove that he can do it.

Kye's story

I come from Peckham in South London originally, where

I was known as the little BMX kid that could always do wheelies.

Now look at me, I've grown up and I'm still growing.

It was tough growing up when and where I did. It obviously wasn't great at times but it made me who I am today. Despite some setbacks and some people not believing in my ability to follow my dreams, I continue to prove everyone wrong.

MY BROTHERS WERE, AND STILL ARE, AN INSPIRATION.

There's my oldest brother, Daniel, who is more than ten years older than me, then Tre, who's six years older than me. When I started secondary school, he was leaving. I never actually crossed paths with anyone that was his age. I took kind of my own path, really. We went to the same school, Peckham Academy. Obviously, my teachers knew Tre. He was good in school anyway; he kept out of trouble.

BMX has always been a family thing.

Tre started first; he'd be with my nan and riding a mountain bike or a BMX bike through Brockwell Park in South London. Then Daniel got involved and then our older sister, Billy, and then I suppose it was my time. You could say it was a rite of passage.

Even from a young age, I was travelling all around the country to compete, probably once or twice a month. It was pretty decent.

We've never actually had any incidents or people being racist towards us in BMX, but when we started out, we were pretty much the only Black people in the sport.

There was Shanaze Reade, the first UK athlete to ride BMX at the Olympics in 2008, and us, really; we were the only Black people in BMX. That was it, literally. I don't believe anyone was racist. My dad's never mentioned it. I don't remember it, so I don't believe anyone's been racist to us.

Thankfully, there's a lot more Black kids involved in the sport now, but there's always room for more.

I would like to think so anyway. At Peckham, we've got over three hundred riders, and obviously most of the kids are Black. It's nice, pretty diverse actually. Black and white kids, and Somalian kids or whatever.

It can be expensive: a beginner's bike is £400. With a helmet and kit, it can cost up to a grand maybe. As a beginner you don't really need to spend that because Peckham, our club, provide helmet, kit and bike, but as you get better and start to enjoy it more, you'll want your own bike. To start off with, this sport was quite cheap, but going to national competitions can be quite expensive for a family – maybe £500, £600 for a weekend, if you include hotel, food, driving up there, paying to race and all that stuff. It's not cheap, but you don't have to go into nationals until you're ready. You can always do regionals. Regionals are a one-day thing, £25 to enter maybe, and the furthest you'll travel is two hours away. It's all pretty close. You don't have to go big straight away if you can't afford it. When you get good enough, you can get a sponsor and they might pay your race fees.

In my first year I was regional champ, national champ, British champ. For me, the journey happened quickly. It was great. I just wanted to meet other kids, race, win and then go home. I was the best in the country. The first time BMX was introduced into the Olympics was 2008, and even at that age, I was like, "Okay, I want to go to the Olympics." I still raced BMX, didn't think anything of it.

Daniel's a rowdy one. He's so rowdy he got kicked off the British team. Maybe a year or two later, Tre was on the team. He went to the Olympics in 2012 as a reserve. That was when I thought, "Okay, I want to do the same thing. Move to Manchester." That's what you do when you join a team, you move to Manchester – home of British Cycling, the sport's governing body – and start training full time. It was 2012, I was twelve or thirteen, and I thought, "That's what I want to do." Not even just because I wanted to do it for myself, but because my older brothers had done it. Then in 2021, when I was twenty-two, I made it to Tokyo.

I was the youngest at that Olympics in BMX, but the oldest was thirty-one. Obviously, he doesn't ride anymore. Once you get to that age, it's kind of like a cut-off point. You can go on if you want to, but the crashing starts to take a toll. It takes longer to come back from injury.

IF SOMEONE TELLS ME I CAN'T DO SOMETHING, I HAVE TO PROVE THEM WRONG.

Tre, he would do well and then he wouldn't do well. Then they're all like, "If you don't do well in this race, then you're off the team." Then he'll do well again. I just made sure that for every race I went to, they couldn't say anything to me. I was always doing my best. They could never give me a reason not to select me for something. I would like to say I made it easy for myself, which is obviously hard to do because it's a sport where other people are trying to do the same thing, but I made sure to show them that I could do it over and over again. I just love proving people wrong!

It's like anything I do in life, I just want to be the best. It feels like a competition to me. I wouldn't compete with my friends over who has the most money or whatever, only with people that feel they can look down on me: "Who are you?" For me, I feel like not even the King can look down on me. I don't really care who you are or anything. If you respect me, I respect you.

I RIDE FOR MY COUNTRY, BUT MAINLY I DO IT FOR ME.

When I got that Olympic silver, people from all different ethnicities were picking me up, just because I represented Britain, and not Jamaica which I could have done. But I've always ridden for the UK. Every time I go to a competition, I'm wearing the national top. My day-to-day life is for the country. I wear the flag on my top now. I mean, if it were easier for me to, I'd probably do it for Jamaica, to be honest, but I'm grateful for all the blessings on this journey so far. When we left school, I wasn't even on a GB team, but I didn't apply for college or anything because I was like, "I'm going to be on the team." It got to a stage where some of my teachers used to tell me, "You might not make it in BMX, you have to do school work, too." I was like, "Okay, I'm definitely going to make it now, just because you said that."

Regardless of whether I was the smartest kid or not, I knew I was going to do BMX. I knew in my mind I was going to make it. If I didn't, it is what it is. School wasn't going to determine whether I made it or not. It's up to me. I didn't really feel the need to go to school. I went, but I didn't care as much as I should have done. It's easy to go down that outsider route, even when I go back to Peckham now.

Getting the medal in Tokyo in 2021 was a great feeling, a proud moment, but the rest of it wasn't quite what I expected. For me, I'd never been to the Olympics before so it was a strange feeling trying to take it all in.

Also, because of COVID, the systems were different to previous Olympic Games. Normally you do your event and then you stay there for the whole thing. You can watch other sports, other people competing, all that stuff. You're partying the whole time. Every night. Whereas, at this Olympics, you do your sport and, whether you get a medal or not, you're going home the next day.

Now that I've done it once, the next Olympics will be even better. In my first one I was distracted the whole time. It was still memorable, but I can't wait to shine at the next one and make my people proud.

Lolly Adefope

I'M A BIT OF EVERYTHING, REALLY

Ololade "Lolly" Adefope is a Black British stand-up comedian and actress specializing in character comedy. When I first met Lolly, I had always been curious about people with names that sounded unmistakably African – Nigerian, in Lolly's case. And curious that her parents had concluded that "Lolly" – as in a lollipop? – would make an excellent name for their child! I understand that in my own culture people are given names, but then as they grow, they're given nicknames or pet names, to use in love and fondness, so it was no big surprise that Lolly's name isn't actually Lolly at all. When she was five years old, one of her friends shortened her name to Lolly, and then over time, everyone started to use Lolly.

I think this is an interesting example about how we as human beings are often trying to make others feel more comfortable, and in doing that we can sometimes sacrifice our own identity. Is it better to go along with simplifying your name rather than having to constantly fight every day to get people to pronounce it correctly? And that's just a simple thing that some of us with names such as Stuart, Hannah, Jordan or Alex don't ever have to think about.

It's always good to expand your understanding and become part of a more diverse world in a community. All of us will have to get better at thinking about how we say someone else's name, especially if we are slightly confused or lack the knowledge to pronounce it correctly.

We need to be better at kindly asking the person how to say their name – after all, their family spent a lot of time choosing it. I remember deciding on my son's name. I know that every name has a meaning, and often those meanings and reasons are quite personal to the person who picked it. This world that we live in provides us with an amazing and significant learning environment, and we all have to find ways to navigate through it so that humans everywhere can become better and more knowledgeable every single day.

IT'S STRANGE GROWING UP AS A BLACK PERSON IN A LARGELY WHITE AREA.

It's hard to escape the stares: wordless but still felt deeply. In the street, on the bus, in school, everywhere you go, people notice. Wherever I went there were always people watching. Sometimes it was like they'd seen a ghost.

I grew up in Sutton, in South London. Some people say it's in Surrey but I suppose it's right on the edge – the story of my life really. Although it doesn't have an Underground station, it does have red buses, just like they do in London. I went to an all-girls' grammar school called Nonsuch High School for Girls, in a place called Cheam.

My childhood was a happy one and for that I am blessed. A standout memory is very simple in many ways, but involves the warmth of family, all four of us – my mum, my dad, my brother and me – huddled up all together in one room. In the living room – my dad watching TV, my mum doing a crossword, and me and my brother both reading. It might not sound like much, but the memory of us all being together is pure heaven to me.

It's a difficult question when asked but I would say I'm British Nigerian, and what makes it extra difficult is the fact that I feel like much more of a Londoner than a Brit. Which may sound strange because my parents were born in Nigeria, but these things can be complicated sometimes, there's always a story to someone's background. My father initially studied in the US, and then studied medicine in Dublin as my grandfather was the Nigerian ambassador to Ireland. My parents met when he was there, then got married in England, and my dad worked as a doctor in London. It's been an international journey to get to where I am today, you could say.

When I was growing up I definitely experienced microaggressions rather than explicit racism. I know it's still going on. Going to a slightly posh all-girls' school, people aren't going to be explicitly racist because they know they're not going to be able to get away with it. But there will be the equivalent in a microaggression.

There were loads of little moments when I was at school, where my friendship group was mainly white. I'd be going about my day thinking that everything is fine and then suddenly someone would make a joke about me being Black or something, and maybe I would go along with the joke if I was in a weird mood.

When it comes down to it, I would say I'm British Nigerian but based in London. I wish there was some way that I could link "Nigerian" and "London" without the "British" because I don't feel particularly British. I guess when I go to America or other countries I feel British. But I feel more like it's the Londoner and the Nigerian that are the most significant parts of me really.

IN MY HEAD, LONDON IS THE COUNTRY THAT I'M FROM.

I definitely feel much more nervous when I'm in other cities. Not necessarily about experiencing racism, but I feel much more aware of being the only Black person in a room. If I have to travel within the UK for work, I may have to go somewhere remote for six weeks and only see three Black people. But I guess whenever I'm not with my friends and family I feel maybe five per cent on edge, whereas in London I feel this is my home. The whole of the city is my house.

I did well at school but then, after my GCSEs, I focused my time and efforts on extracurricular activities. My A Levels were not quite as good as my GCSEs, but at this age I was starting to think about and experiment with comedy. My dad was a surgeon and I've met many doctors and surgeons before who've been like, "Wow I can't believe that you get up on stage and try and make people laugh." I'm like, "But you're a surgeon!" So I definitely see their jobs as much more noble and important, and they have much more of an impact and help the country in many more ways than I could ever do. Then I remember that not everyone can be a doctor, or wants to be a doctor; there is room for all types of skills and talents to shine. To be honest, those nimble-fingered surgeons also need time to relax and be entertained and switch off, and that's where comedy comes in.

WE'VE GOT FAMILY EVERYWHERE.

I have uncles and aunties and cousins back in Africa, and a lot of my cousins live in London, some of them live in Canada; my dad's brother lives in New York – so not always the easiest destinations to travel to. My family are pretty spread out now, you could say.

I do like how varied our journeys have been. It can be hard to be pigeonholed into particular boxes, but I would pick African if I had to define myself a certain way. Sometimes questionnaires and forms can be tricky and it's hard to know the point of them. I would tick Black African or Black British, but this feels like a label that someone else is giving me in order to understand where I'm from, not something that I necessarily associate with. "How can I fit you into a box of people?"

A number of times, I've overheard something and I've doubted whether that was really said. Even in my adult life I've overheard someone say something offensive and I've been like, they can't have really said that. I've gone over it in my head and thought, No, no they didn't. Then I'll message someone later on and say, "Did you hear that?" They'll be like, "Yes, I did hear that." But very often nobody else brings it up. I could have convinced myself it didn't happen, but it definitely did.

It's important to be careful with what you say – you don't know who you're talking to.

You don't know who might be offended by it and who is just staying silent because they might feel uncomfortable or triggered. I think it's increasingly important to be more mindful and respectful when telling a joke; we are all humans after all and deserve the same level of respect.

Why would you go into this industry

if you didn't want to be REALLY GOOD at it?

It's a dream job, one that many people want to do from a young age. Why would you not try your hardest? You might as well just not do it. I wonder if that is linked to coming from a family of high achievers and feeling like if I'm going to do this, I'm going to do it properly.

I'M A BIT OF EVERYTHING, REALLY.

Sometimes I don't really know where different elements of my personality come from. I suppose it comes from my youth, my parents; me and my brother were brought up to be ambitious and work hard at school – ninety nine per cent wasn't good enough, it had to be one hundred per cent. I think that is definitely a Nigerian mentality. I'm also a Virgo, which means that I'm a perfectionist. So does that come from my star sign or does that come from the fact that I'm Nigerian?

It was during the Coronavirus pandemic especially that I realized that people play their parts to help in different ways, for example, by making people laugh and keeping them entertained during the toughest of times. There are bigger things in life to worry about and the pandemic showed us all that. But then at the same time it's nice to recognize that comedy does help people who are doing the real work, and it does give people a form of escapism and a chance to unwind. And TV is an accessible form of that for people.

I tend to be in a lot of quite heartwarming TV shows, and that feels like I'm putting something nice into the world.

It was really my brother who got me into comedy,

and music too, to be honest. All of my cultural tastes have been formed through either what he recommended to me or me trying to impress him. Even now we tease each other about who introduced whom to what and who was the first person to listen. But maybe there's just an interesting bond between an older brother and a younger sister. Even now, he's still very protective of me and I want to impress him, but there's not really competition. When we were younger we used to argue all the time, but it was all love. We're just very close and have a lot of similar tastes. We're also two people who both grew up in London, are aware that we're Nigerian and have a deep-rooted connection to Nigeria, but deep inside, despite all the difficulties, we have to admit that we are, of course, British too.

Kwajo
Tweneboa

IT'S ALL ABOUT CHANGING THE NARRATIVE ... AND HERE'S HOW MINE STARTS

We are all born with a gift to do something to help Earth become a better place. We can spend a lifetime trying to find that fantastic, unique thing. Apart from Kwajo Tweneboa, I don't know anyone other than myself who found their calling at such a young age. Questions mean answers, and I believe that young Kwajo found a way of asking the right questions, to get justice for himself and for others in similar situations.

Kwajo Tweneboa has gone from a determined social housing tenant to a viral nationwide housing campaigner, after posting videos of his living conditions on social media. After going through something as traumatic as losing his father, while living in a dire housing situation, Kwajo became a champion for change and for highlighting plight of others. He sees it as his mission to ensure that he speaks for those who feel they have no voice. He doesn't mind who he upsets, offends or causes to feel slightly uncomfortable while striving for safe living conditions for all.

From a simple start to a fantastic future, I'm sure that he will continue to mature, and he will use his experiences growing up in London to help him in the work he does today.

MY NAME IS KWAJO LEON TWENEBOA,

AND THE IDEA OF HOME HAS BEEN IMPORTANT TO ME SINCE YOUTH.

The famous saying states

"Home is where the heart is."

In my line of work that couldn't be more true.

I've been busy lately, it never stops. Running around but also being given the run-around by housing associations when all I want to do is help. Being a voice for people who do not have a voice, or worse, who do not have a liveable home to be in.

I don't know how I survived primary school because I wasn't the best student I could have been. I think I was misunderstood by many. I could be a menace at times; I was turning over tables, I was fighting kids.

I admit that I struggled with the intensity of school and the heaviness of trying to be me within a confined environment. I don't really understand it, but being told you can't do certain things or being controlled –

I don't think I liked that, and I used to take it out in the classrooms. "I'm not listening, you can't convince me otherwise." I used to have fights with the boys in the class. I remember this one boy, we used to fight pretty much every day. I was a real problem for the teachers. Even the headteachers, the deputy heads. The headteacher got it and thought it was coming from somewhere, but neither of us knew where that place was.

I remember I found school hard in those early years, but then I changed schools and I was the complete opposite. I remember one of the teachers at my new school saying, "Oh, I read your report..." This was a few weeks in. "I can't believe you're the same person, that you were having fights and getting into all this trouble." I don't know why but that really, really stuck, and from then I kind of continued on that sort of well-behaved journey, trying to keep my head down and do the work my teacher set me. Soon enough, I went from being behind others in my class – like, a year, in terms of development – to being back level with them.

Then secondary school was just fun. I wasn't badly behaved in the sense of what I was when I was younger, but there were times where I was mischievous, you could say. I used to joke around, but it was never something where I'd be getting into daily fights. I'd snapped out of that behaviour. I got on well with my teachers. I'm friends with some of them even now.

I GET ON WITH ALL THE TEACHERS THAT GOT ON WITH ME.

And the teaching assistants too. The TAs had a lot of patience and would talk to you and speak with you. Even if you were misbehaving or whatever, they had that time. Whereas, sometimes I could be quite argumentative with the teachers I didn't get on with. But I suppose it comes down to that whole thing of constantly being told you're wrong. It's like, "I'm going to continue being the opposite to what you want, and if you're labelling me this sort of way, I'm going to play up to that role."

Later on, I learned that was a self-fulfilling prophecy.

When you're constantly telling a young person they're bad and they're the ones misbehaving, they're always starting things, they're the ones that are constantly reprimanded even though they may be right in certain situations, then they're going to live up to that role. They're only young and they're still learning, and that's the same for a lot of young people. I was sort of lucky in the sense that I became strong, was able to snap out of that, because a lot of people carried that on through secondary school and beyond into adult life.

THERE WAS A BIG SHIFT.

Had I gone to secondary school with the same attitude I had in primary school, I could have been in a completely different situation now. I would have almost certainly been a very different person. But these experiences have shaped who I am, the foundations I'm building for myself.

Being British is hard to define. We've got the Royal Family and a flag that we wave around every now and again, but there's nothing much that I would take from that. Whereas, with my dad and Ghana, that means a lot more. There's history there, there's very much a culture. I'm sure they still have traditional ways of doing things, and I'll see that when I go there; he's talked a lot about Ghana but we've never managed to go. It's the same with my mum, that idea of religion and history in Ireland; there's a lot there too.

My mum's from a place called Galway, and Ireland as a nation has a difficult and bloody history. It's weird because although I was born in the UK, I feel like I understand and get the sort of cultures from the other two places: Ireland and Ghana. In many ways, I understand their cultures better than my own. She often mentions the Troubles and everything, talks about the famines, religion, how there are strict Catholics where she's from and what it's like to grow up in that sort of environment.

Whenever anyone asks me, "Where are you from?" I automatically assume they mean, "Where are your parents from?" And I say Ghana and Ireland, although

I'm British. Again, my passport says British. I just feel more pride for the other two places, and a disconnect when it comes to being from here. I hope that changes. Hopefully a leader comes along that will make me feel proud of that again.

I want to go to Ghana soon,

maybe even live there one day. The blazing sun to lift my spirits and leave me in a better mood all day, what more could anyone want? That said, I do consider myself British – Black British and proud. It's just a fact that I am, but if someone was to ask what that means – it's a tough question and the answer is complex. Whereas, if I was to ask my dad that, or someone from the Caribbean or any other country, they'd know what to say. They'd know what their history meant and feel a positivity about their country of birth that I can't muster.

There's a lot of things about this country that I just don't stand with or stand for. There's still a lot of things I don't understand. Sometimes it feels like we're going backwards, whether it be politics and the people in control of the country, basically any one with influence. We see so much suffering – it shouldn't be happening. This isn't a place that I feel you can be proud of. It's disappointing to say, because I know we call ourselves Great Britain, with a question mark hovering over the "Great" part of it. People should be allowed to feel a part of the country that they're living in.

My parents drilled the idea of hard work into me, you could say, because they were key workers for the majority of their working life. They worked with the elderly, looking after others, and that is something that has always inspired me. I remember visiting the hospital when my dad was ill. I think about it quite a lot. When he was in hospital, he was so ill he couldn't walk. He was using a Zimmer frame and he was very, very weak and bedbound. He was being fed through a tube into his stomach. There were times when he was very forgetful. He used to repeat things, and he'd tell the nurse, "I used to do this job. I used to look after the sick."

He didn't want to be so ill. Probably didn't feel like he was ready to be in that situation yet. He had worked so hard all his life. He had two caring jobs at once. In the morning he would drop us off at school and then go and do his morning work at Age Concern, looking after elderly people. Later he would come and pick us up and then nap for a few hours before going off again to his evening job, where he would go from client to client, looking after them, giving them their medication. I remember him always filling out these pink timesheets, piles of them. So he was very hardworking. My mum too. She was doing the same. That's where they met – they were both carers at the same place. Hard work and caring for others were in their blood.

Caring for others, especially those who are vulnerable, that's clearly something that they passed on to me through the work they were doing. Along with the whole caring side of it, it's about fighting injustice, standing up, being frustrated and not taking no for an answer. That's very much me, showing other young people of colour that can be the case, no matter your background, no matter your history, no matter what you're told about stereotypes. Ultimately, your voice does matter and you do have that power to influence change.

I would call myself a young Black male from a working-class background. It's complicated, it always is, but who's to question how I feel? I've had this discussion before: I identify as Black because if I go to a European country like Switzerland, they're going to say, "You're Black." Whether you like it or not they will just tell you, "You're Black." I know my mum's white, and I'm not going to deny having that side of me, but I identify as Black because of my background, where I'm from, and the fact that I grew up largely around my dad's culture. He was a Ghanaian man and I'm a direct descendant of that. I'm very much surrounded by culture – not just African, but Caribbean culture too.

People forget about the cultural side of things – your background and what it truly means to be a person of colour or Black. The weight of it, the pride that should be felt. That's why I argue that point. I've got it from both sides. I've had white people say, "No, you're Black," and then I've had Black people say, "Well, you're not Black. You're mixed race." That's another thing. A whole other conversation about mixed race people and the fact that in some cases you're never accepted on either side. That connection with my dad, with my mum, being from a working-class background, being from an estate. I'm proud of all these things. So that's how I'd describe myself.

I want to inspire other people like me, other Black individuals who are from disadvantaged backgrounds. I want to be able to show them that I'm a part of that, and show them just how important their voices are and how much they mean and how proud they should feel. No matter what background you're from, no matter what your past, whether you're from a disadvantaged background, whether you couldn't afford things when you were a child, and you weren't able to have the luxuries of other demographics.

It's not until you get older that you realize your parents did the best that they could do, and mine honestly did that. I'm very lucky to be able to say that because there are a lot of people out there that can't, or don't have both parents in their lives, so I'm also very, very lucky to have had the parents that I have. I just hope that Dad's able to see everything I do. It's a nice thought that even when a parent passes away they can still see that. My mum gets to see it. She gets to see all of it. She can't keep up with all the work I'm trying to do.

I JUST WANT ALL OF MY FAMILY TO STILL BE HERE AND HAVE GOOD HEALTH.

That's the priority over everything else. For myself too, to have good health, that's number one. One thing I've realized is that health is the most important and valuable thing that anyone can have, because without good health you've got nothing. Secondly, just to be able to look back in ten years and say, "Well done, Kwajo, you made the change you wanted to. What you did in the beginning, putting your foot down, was the right thing to do, and ultimately you've indirectly helped so many others as a result of that."

It's all about changing the

narrative ... and here's how mine starts.

I've grown up in social housing the majority of my life. For the most part, the experience wasn't great. I've lived in homes that were literally falling apart and we were constantly being ignored by landlords. One time, we were living in a converted car garage; it still had the garage door on. No one should've been living in there. Pipes burst during winter and flooded the whole place. No furniture. It was damp. There was mould growing on the bed. I'm sure it was illegal, it was that bad.

MY DAD WAS FIGHTING FOR YEARS FOR A PERMANENT PLACE, AND EVENTUALLY WE MOVED.

But the bad news is that this place was worse. Yes, the house was bigger and fitted us all in, but it was just in a complete state of disrepair. We had light fittings filled with water. We had mice, we had cockroaches. We had kitchen cupboards that were nearly one hundred years old. A bathroom that wasn't fit for use. I was having to take showers in a gym. We had windows that were broken. Our back door, the fences, our front door even, were all broken. Someone tried to break in at one point using a crowbar, but they could've just walked in the back if they'd gone around there. At one point, it was missing parts of the ceiling for more than six months.

It was a living hell, to be honest.

No one should have been living in that place. I remember workmen coming in and saying, "I don't mean to offend you, but not even animals should be living here," and it was at that point that I thought, *This is bad. This is really, really bad.* Our landlord was just ignoring us. I'd had enough. Ultimately, I said, enough's enough. So I went around the house, took pictures, uploaded it to social media, and millions of people saw it. After all of that, after the pictures, the mice, the cockroaches, you name it, the landlord was still in denial.

So then I went around every single home on my whole estate and did the exact same. Collected evidence and uploaded it to social media, which again was shared even more. It was picked up by ITV News, who broadcast it. It was actually a top story that day. You can even hear, listening back to the recordings of it, how disgusted the presenters were that this was going on. You can hear it in their voices. Then I went around the estates in my local area and did the same because they were falling apart too. I was getting people living under different housing providers reaching out to me from across London, asking me to help by using my growing platform. So I went and did the same for them. Going to other people's homes, travelling across London, using my own student loan money to pay for it. And now I'm going around the country. I'm trying to get change at government level. Through social media, they're very aware of the work that I'm doing. Hopefully now, systematic change will come from the top – real change. Real change is what I'm driving for.

EVERY CHILD DOES MATTER.

Sometimes people forget, politicians especially, that they're overlooking the harm done to children by poor housing. As it stands, substandard housing is not considered a children's safeguarding issue. So kids living in terrible conditions, moving from hotel to hotel and falling behind with work even during their GCSEs, it's not considered an issue by schools. That just goes to show how these kids have been completely ignored and that's what needs to change. They need to be massively prioritized for safeguarding.

Alison Hammond

TO
ME,
FAMILY
IS
EVERYTHING

I'm old enough to remember when reality TV first burst onto our TV screens and was the genre watched in all households. It was in the third series of *Big Brother* in 2002 that Alison first appeared on television. Since then, she has been able to cement herself into the very core of popular culture and is now a presenter on the flagship ITV breakfast show, *This Morning*.

Her hometown of Birmingham is known as the heart of the West Midlands. As a child, I visited friends and family who lived in this area and I had many a happy weekend there playing with my cousins and their friends. I have always seen it as quite a multicultural, accepting place, even though I know there have been troubled times, and that there were many protests in the 1970s and '80s against racist immigration laws. Alison's outlook of what it was like to be growing up Black in the Midlands has opened my eyes and given me a better understanding about the UK overall. It's easy for me to feel like the London experience is unique and, in many ways, easier for Black people due to the city being more diverse. This perceived "easier" experience is not always the case in other places, which is why it's so important to hear from Black people who grew up all around the country.

Other people will always have opinions on who they think you are. Alison is an example to us all, showing that other people's thoughts have nothing to do with where you will go and how far you can push yourself.

Alison's story

Birmingham is known as the "Second City" because it's the second biggest city in the UK. To me, though, it will always be number one. My home. The place that raised me and gave me what I needed to be me. The city that made me who I am today, the woman I'm proud to be.

I grew up in a place called Kingstanding, Birmingham, with my mum, brother and sister. It wasn't always easy. My mum was a single parent, juggling many jobs to keep us warm, well-fed and happy. She often got help from family, the community and her friends. But, when it comes down to it, she raised the three of us.

I was born and brought up in Britain, but both my parents are from Jamaica. As such, I feel I have really strong ties to Jamaica: the people, the good vibes and the sense of belonging I feel when I visit, and from hearing stories from my mum about her childhood there and how much she loved the country when she was growing up. However, I have always said I'm Black British. My mum came here to join her mum in Leeds aged eight. It took two weeks on a ship with her grandmother. My mum told me she was sick the whole journey and could only manage to eat Maria biscuits.

I went to Cardinal Wiseman Roman Catholic school. It was a multicultural school and my schoolfriends were some of the nicest people I've ever known. My standout childhood memory is family mainly, being all together in front of the TV. Mum in the kitchen cooking ackee and saltfish. Me watching Saturday morning TV shows like *CD:UK* with Ant and Dec, *Desmond's*, *GMTV*, *Press Gang*, *Neighbours*. Just family being all around and the smell of great cooking.

There is the expectation that you have to be a bubbly, larger-than-life character when you're on TV, but you still need support. Culture and heritage to me means family, friends, food, music and language. I'm proud of my roots and how they have shaped me to become the person I am today. Family always comes first, and then you have the friends who become like an extended family. Then the food and music bring everyone together. And when you are in the comfort of your family and friends, you speak a language that is only understood by those who love you. That for me is culture and heritage because it's what I was brought up seeing and what I continue to do in my life.

To me, family is everything.

I have two half-sisters who live out in Jamaica. Whenever I go back to see them, I feel this connection, all warm and fuzzy inside. I feel this natural sense of belonging, like I should be there. Everyone is the same as you, you don't stand out. It just feels like I belong.

My mum always carried through Jamaican elements into our lives: the food, the culture, the music and the language were always around me, so it gave me a sense of pride and made me feel like, even though I was in Birmingham, I was Jamaican.

I don't often feel like I'm different when I'm in Britain, or maybe I don't notice it as I don't like to focus on differences. Don't get me wrong, sometimes I do look around and realize that I'm the only Black person in certain spaces, and to be honest, sometimes I don't really mind. But when I'm in Jamaica, I naturally fit in. I realize that I'm not different there, so I feel more different when I come back to England.

I do feel safe and comfortable here in Britain, but it's just every now and again when I notice that I'm different. I'm Black first and British second. I feel like just being me makes me Black and British. Asking someone who is Black British what makes them British almost implies they aren't British to start off with.

TO ME, TO BE BLACK AND BRITISH MEANS THAT'S EXACTLY WHAT I AM.

Whenever I have to tick "Other" on a form about racial identity, it makes me feel like I really am someone "other".

For me, the murder of George Floyd was a big moment. That was the first time I really noticed that I was an "other"; the only Black person in the room. I suddenly went from being just me to being an expert on all things "Black". I was the person everyone would turn to, and was almost expected to speak up and share my thoughts and feelings, reliving any traumas and fears for my son, brother, family and friends. It was and still is a lot to carry on your shoulders and it was slightly traumatic, but I knew it was something I had to do so people knew the truth, my truth.

I love Jamaican food, but I also like to add my English heritage into the mix; you could call them "Jamlish" meals. Music is also important to me, from my mum playing reggae when I was growing up to my son listening and teaching me all about grime and hip hop. And it's really important to me to keep speaking Patois. Speaking it and hearing it not only reminds me of my mum, it also makes me feel closer to Jamaica.

I believe doing my job highlights my culture because it helps with representation, showing people the best of Black Britishness, the best of Birmingham. Whenever I'm on TV, I'm always my true authentic self, and that's the best way to be, professionally and personally: I cry, I laugh, and I do it all with my Brummie accent.

I believe me being on screen shows young Black people their dreams can be achieved, no matter where they come from, or what accent they have.

I am currently writing a book called *Black in Time*, looking at Black figures, icons, trailblazers throughout time, so the next generation can learn and own a piece of history that I was never taught.

I feel like I contribute authentic true Black joy and happiness to everyone from every race. I believe that by being my real self on TV it lets people into my real life, my culture and heritage. It shows them how positive I am, and we try to do the same as a family too.

But the most important thing for me is legacy. I hope that by doing the job that I do, speaking up on the topics and issues I do, shining a light on the struggle we can face as Black people at times, sharing my culture and love for family, it helps people have an understanding, and through that contributes to the future being better. I try to be part of the change and hope that I'm successful.

My mum, Maria, is the trunk of my family tree; she stood tall and strong so we could all blossom. A force of nature, a strong Black Jamaican woman who moved to a new country, then raised her children as a single mum, all with a smile on her face and God in her heart. She is me, and I am her on so many levels. I fully embody her.

She impacted and still impacts every aspect of my life every day. She was an amazing cook and I got my kitchen skills from her. She had a very strong faith, and so do I.

She also sometimes – not often – had a temper, which I can have sometimes. But through her teachings, that rarely is the case now.

Her love for me and our family cannot be put into words. She taught me about love, family, food and music – all the best things in life. All these things are important in my life and that is because of her. She was and always will be my guiding light, and although I am growing and developing, she is always in me.

I am many things to different people, but I'm proud to be from Birmingham, proud to be a Brummie woman of Jamaican heritage.

Eunice Olumide

I GENUINELY WALK THROUGH LIFE WITHOUT JUDGING PEOPLE

Eunice Olumide MBE is a Scottish fashion model and actress, as well as being a TV presenter and DJ.

Other people's assumptions and perceptions are something that Eunice has had to deal with for a large part of her life. That's one of the major reasons why I wanted to write this book and talk about this with her, in order for all of us to better understand the unique challenges that we each face in life. It's what we then do with this knowledge that's important; we can reduce our own assumptions and stop putting people in boxes, just to make ourselves feel more comfortable.

We put people in boxes because it makes us feel easier about being ourselves, and the more we understand this, the better the world will be.

It would be great if we all could reflect on that before we open our mouths to give opinions about people we may or may not know. It's a difficult task, I know, but I will continue trying to live my life that way!

I remember being young and Black in Scotland and enjoying that beautiful, innocent bliss of childhood.

However, as I got older, things slowly started to change. The older I got, I gradually discovered how difficult it was for some people to accept me as a Black person. Essentially, in a world where skin colour shouldn't matter, to too many people it did.

As a child – like most other children, I expect – I wasn't really aware of people's skin colour because my feeling is, we're all human after all, aren't we? But sometimes that message of humanity and togetherness doesn't find its way through to people's minds, and because of that I suffered sometimes. Well, quite a lot actually.

So after a peaceful and innocent start, as I got older, things started to change and my Black skin caused a reaction in certain people that I hadn't seen before. People started to look at me a different way. In fact, by the time I was eight, nine, ten, eleven years old I became conscious that I wasn't always allowed to hang out with other kids. Why? One reason: because I was Black.

These moments of judgement and being made to feel different have stayed with me all my life and shape the way I think about the world as a Black woman living in Britain today.

It wasn't easy, and that's putting it lightly.

It's been a long journey and sometimes I have found myself all at sea trying to figure it all out.

I should probably start with how my family ended up in Scotland. My dad was in the navy and that's what brought him to the UK. To be honest, as beautiful as my country is, I don't think he or any of my family really knew the type of abuse they would face just for being Black. Speaking honestly and from the heart as I always do, the treatment we got sometimes was extreme, like something from a Hollywood horror movie: our house was regularly trashed, spray-painted and defaced, and even burned down by vandals. We were getting attacked physically by gangs of youths with golf clubs. I admit, it was really scary sometimes and I had to grow up faster than I wanted to just to stay alive, just to survive.

GROWING UP, MY MUM WAS – AND STILL IS – A HUGE SOURCE OF INSPIRATION TO ME.

She used to work at the High Commission and she strived so hard to provide for us. I remember she had three jobs when I was at school to ensure she set the right example and offered us the best opportunities. Through her, I was always taught you just need to work hard to do well in life. She has this powerful African spirit, which sometimes I find worrying, especially as she gets older. She still never stops. One day I asked her why she doesn't slow down, and she was like, "Well, in Nigeria, we say if you stay still or lie down, you might not get back up."

Growing up in a place like Scotland is very difficult

because the experience of being Black isn't always the same as when you're Black and come from England.

In many ways, I think it was worse. Living north of the border, as they call it, we didn't have a whole community of Black people to turn to, no close-knit circle of Black families to share our experiences with, no special membership, no support network to talk to and help protect us. There were no large groups of Black people that I could really identify with, or that I could go to and talk about the trauma that I was suffering.

SOMETIMES BEING BLACK AND SCOTTISH ISN'T APPRECIATED.

In the same way that the USA overshadows Canada across the pond, England dominates everything here in the UK: jobs, education, arts, media, broadcasting and fashion.

Sometimes as a young Scottish person, Black or white, you're led to believe that you're inferior, not good or special enough, that your accent is wrong. I see it too often, sometimes when I watch films or a much-loved television show; the Scottish characters are often seen as slightly strange. The butt of the joke. The silly ones who are always made fun of. This isn't fair. I'm now trying to do my bit to change people's idea of Scottish people. I've made TV shows just to show people, children in particular, that our stories, told in our own accents, do exist and they do matter. Scottish children are constantly seeing English people on their screens, and I know of many kids who are petrified that they won't be taken seriously or get their dream job because they don't speak with an English accent. We need to show the world that isn't the case. I've too often been told that the way I speak is wrong because it's not the "King's English". It might seem obvious, but people from Scotland deserve to be respected too.

It's a personal mission of mine to change people's perspectives about being Black and Scottish.

Growing up in Scotland is seen by some to be not as glamorous as growing up in England. But I, and many others, turned out just fine, and it's my goal to showcase how special Scotland is and how wonderful the people who live there are too. I admit, being one of only a few Black people in a country as white as Scotland, it was tough at times to push through the stares and glares and judgement, and it still is. But I want to play my part in taking a stand for what I believe in and helping to ensure we all get along without the much-too-high barriers and unfair criticism.

Sometimes in the various industries I have been involved in, there haven't been any others who looked like me. Growing up, there were no role models I could really look up to. That's mainly because there haven't been many successful Black people who were given the chance to shine, especially outside London. I'm determined to continue flying the flag for those who call themselves Black and Scottish.

Because our story is just as valid as far as I am concerned.

SOMETIMES PEOPLE FORGET SCOTLAND'S HISTORY IS JUST AS RICH AS ENGLAND'S.

They get themselves stuck in their own little bubble and find it hard to see beyond their own beliefs. In other countries, some people I speak to don't believe me when I tell them that there are Black people in the UK who don't live in London, even though I'm a living example standing right in front of them.

So, I'm on a mission – yes, a quest, you could say.

Some people are intimidated by the fact that I stand up for myself as a Black Scottish woman, with strong beliefs about who I am and where I come from, and sometimes I miss opportunities because I'm considered a little too outspoken. Fair enough. I've never been afraid to speak about what I believe in.

I'M SCOTTISH AND PROUD, BUT I WILL NEVER FORGET MY ROOTS.

I'm the first generation of my family to be born outside of Africa, so you could definitely say that I identify as an African and a Scot. Nearly all my family are in Africa, which is a blessing, but quite isolating too because they are so far away. I've been to Nigeria many times, and I think that Africa is the best place in the world. It's hard to explain but when I go to Africa, I feel normal, free from the judgement that can weigh heavy sometimes. Even though I have a Scottish accent and that makes me stand out in some places, there is a freedom I feel there that loosens all the pressures on my shoulders.

Being Black and Scottish in England is so rare. Black English people, regardless of how much money they've got, think of Scotland as cold and racist. To them, it's just a little town, not an actual country. Or even a place that doesn't exist at all.

In all honesty, it's hard to define what being British means. It's confusing and perplexing at times, hard to put my finger on an exact definition. But I'm not British really, I'm not English, I'm not Anglo, or Irish, or Welsh. I'm Nigerian but I just happened to be born and raised in Scotland, so I'm certainly Scottish too. In fact, I coined the term Afro-Scot when I was sixteen. So, that's what I identify as, an Afro-Scot.

Despite my Scottish accent, English people often forget that I'm not from England and I don't think the same as them; I don't find the same things funny, and I don't identify. So, when I meet English people, it's usually really cool at first, but then because I'm Scottish, they start to judge me.

There are some funny situations where being Black and Scottish really surprises people. I'll be trying to buy a bus ticket and at first the driver will be really angry, and he's looking at me thinking, *You're English, right?* And he's quite rude to me, like, "What's wrong with you, man? You're supposed to have an Oyster before you get on the bus, what's wrong with you?" "I'm really sorry," I say, "I'm not from this country," and they're like, "Oh, sorry, sorry, sorry. Oh my God, you're from Scotland. They've got Black people in Scotland?" It's a big issue because this often happens to me in cities — not just London, but New York, Paris.

I feel judged

by at least ten people a day.

And the thing is, I don't get upset because they're not me, and they haven't had the same experience as me. Obviously we're programmed to make a judgement about someone within the first thirty seconds or after hanging out with them once, which is the done thing in this country. Whereas in Scotland, that's not how things are done. It's only after at least the third meeting that you can really form an opinion because there's nothing you can learn about someone the first time. Unless you're having a really in-depth conversation where you're asking them specific questions – then you can make certain judgements.

I genuinely walk through life without judging people

but it seems I don't get the pleasure of that same treatment. It's like every day of my life someone is judging me. When I meet humans, I don't do that, and that's why knowledge is important. Knowledge and acceptance.

IT'S TIME TO CHANGE THE NARRATIVE, AND I WILL CONTINUE TO PLAY MY PART.

Patrice Lawrence

MY EARLIEST MEMORIES ARE OF GROWING UP AROUND LOVE

Patrice Lawrence MBE is a Black British writer and journalist who has published fiction for adults and children. Children can be so resilient; they can often endure far beyond what they should have to, because they have no other life experience to help them set the bar for what is "normal" and what is not. Patrice's story of her childhood is a humbling example of the way the world was in the early seventies and how other people and stigmas can have such a profound effect on one's sense of self.

Think about growing up only seeing faces that don't look like you at all. How might that make you feel? Why are you the only one to experience the inquisitiveness and interrogation from others, curious prodding, stroking, pulling, touching your skin, asking why you are different? We could spin this into a positive and say uniqueness is valued and admired. But the younger we are, the less we understand that fact, so Patrice's early years of life sound very tough and challenging. For her to come out the other side as such a lovely, warm, kind, giving, curious, fantastic person after such a traumatic early childhood experience – well, it's just a testament to who she is as a person and to both her mum and foster mum, Auntie Phyllis.

Some of the challenges that Patrice has faced over her lifetime are extraordinary, and this is, in my opinion, why she has gone on to be such a fantastic writer with such a glorious and expansive imagination.

Patrice's story

You could say that my story is a little complicated,

and being a writer, I know all about a complex story or two. So, where to begin? With my family, I suppose. My mum was born in Trinidad. She was the second youngest of twelve – well, twelve surviving – so I reckon my grandma must've been pregnant for every one of her childbearing days.

My mum's older sister, my auntie, organized for my mum to come to the UK and train to be a psychiatric nurse in Brighton.

Sussex was very white.

My biological dad, Patrick, was born in Guyana and brought up in Barbados. I think he had quite a troubled life. His mum was Indian and his father was African-Guyanese. There was stigma about being biracial, and about being a child of unmarried parents. So he ended up in Brighton to train to be a psychiatric nurse. I only got a photo of him very recently. My dad was incredibly handsome, and I learned that he was one of the first Black psychiatric nurses at this big hospital in Sussex. He cut a swathe through the other nurses because he was so good-looking – and unfaithful to my mum, from what I understand.

So, when my mum fell pregnant, her choices were limited. Being Black, unmarried and pregnant was a difficult place to be in 1960s Britain. She hadn't finished training to be a nurse, so her options were to send me to Trinidad to be looked after by one of my aunties, or to have the pregnancy terminated, which was still illegal. Or I could have been adopted, and a lot of people my age were adopted because their parents weren't married – the stigma of being born 'out of wedlock' was that great.

My mum didn't do any of those things. Instead, I was privately fostered in a place called Whitehawk, near Brighton, from the age of four months to four years. It was a white working-class family: my foster mum, Auntie Phyllis, and her two much older children, Linda and Terry. She taught to me to read when I was very little, joined me up to a library and even into my twenties she would send me books of poetry, including works by Yeats. There were lots of day trips. I suppose she just encouraged me to be a curious child and to learn.

MY EARLIEST MEMORIES ARE OF GROWING UP AROUND LOVE,

but of course, growing up in the seventies, you're also aware of your differences too. I may be a writer, but there is no word for that feeling, that tension that exists when people see you and you're trying to work out what they think about you.

I went back to live with my mum when I was four, and I quite often say that one of my earliest memories is that day she came to collect me, knowing I wasn't going to live with my auntie anymore. I was just crying and crying and crying, and they both agreed that I should not see my auntie for a while until I settled down with my mum.

My mum is a massive reader, absolutely massive, and it's funny, my daughter talks about people's love languages, and me and my mum's love language is books. We still send each other books now. My mum read lots of what I suppose people call the classics, so I kind of had this strange relationship with reading. Even now, she'll read a book and give it to me and we'll talk about it, and that was how we bonded back then. My mum loves the romantic poets, Keats, Wordsworth and Tennyson, and also the novels *Anne of Green Gables* and *Little Women*, so I read all of those, took them all in.

BUT EVERY BOOK WAS TELLING ME THAT PEOPLE LIKE ME DON'T WRITE BOOKS AND AREN'T IN BOOKS.

From Brighton I went to a place called Haywards Heath. It's south of London, between Gatwick and Brighton. It's not very exciting, although a lot of Londoners are moving down there now, including those of colour. By then my mum met my stepdad, Angelo, who is Italian. There's a stereotype about Italians having slightly tanned skin. Angelo never got the memo. He has brought me up since I was four, so always introduces me as his daughter. People look at him and they look at me, and look at my mum, if she's there, and try and work out how they can politely comment on our lack of family resemblance.

My mum and Angelo got married when I was about nine and had my two younger brothers. We're all different colours, all of us, so as well as living somewhere that's predominantly white with a family that nobody could quite work out, we were never like the families in the books that I read. So you think there's something wrong with you in a way. And I wasn't seeing myself in the books that I loved so much – I just wasn't there.

In *The Story of Doctor Dolittle*, that Hugh Lofting wrote and illustrated, Dr Dolittle goes to Africa, and that's never going to end well. One of the characters is called Prince Bumpo (really, Hugh?), and his storyline is that to get the princess, he has to bleach himself white! I read that when I was six. There were still books like *Little Black Sambo* around when I was a kid and golliwog dolls. I absorbed all these racist messages about where I belonged in the world. I never thought that I could grow up to be an author.

My secondary school was in a village called Cuckfield. It was a school of around 1,700 students, and roughly ten of us weren't white. I was quite academic, and my mum's colonial British education helped me, especially with the English literature and history curriculum, so I did quite well. I had a couple of amazing English teachers in the second and third year; they were newly qualified when they taught me. Then, when *Orangeboy* won awards, they both found me on social media. They congratulated me and told me that they always thought I could be a writer, and I really appreciated being able to thank them for my support.

My biological father is one of the reasons I write a lot about bereavement and sadness in my books. Patrick Edward Singh is someone I never lived with, but I did get to know him; I used to go and visit him in his Brighton basement flat, crammed with guitars and books. He was really into science fiction, which is why I gave that enthusiasm to Marlon and his deceased dad in *Orangeboy*. I've read so many of Isaac Asimov's books because my dad recommended them. He was a great *Star Trek* fan too; the TV series and their novelizations! He tried to persuade me to read Kafka, Hemingway and Herman Hesse as well as Richard Bach's *Jonathan Livingstone Seagull*.

Sadly, he failed. Though he did buy me my first Alice Walker book – *The Color Purple*.

He fell out of my life for for eleven years, but when I was around twenty he got in touch with me. I used to go and see him in Brighton. He had some mental health issues and he was bouncing between squats and hostels. From what I know now, his old nursing friends reached out and tried to help him, so he wasn't completely abandoned. He sent me a birthday card for my twenty-first birthday and said he was moving on from the hostel where he was staying, and would be in contact with me again when he was more settled. Then I heard no more from him.

A couple of years later, I heard that he had died in a fire in a squat. I just didn't know how to process it. I went to work the next day. There was one other Black guy at work – he was my friend, and he phoned the coroner for me. Apparently, the police had been sent round to inform me, but couldn't find my address. I lived in a small cul-de-sac of thirty-one homes – many of us moved there at the same time and me and my mum were the only Black people. I was easy to find.

Worse was to come. I phoned the coroner several times to ask about funeral arrangements. They advised me to let the council organize it because of the costs. I'd said that I'd wanted to be there. Someone ticked the wrong box. The last time that I phoned for an update, they told me that the funeral had happened. Because my dad was a Black man, somebody who was an alcoholic, somebody who was homeless, I felt that he was treated with no compassion. There must have been a deeply ingrained assumption that nobody cared about him. Even though this was thirty-odd years ago, I'm still furious about it. I don't know if anybody was there at his funeral. God knows where his ashes are or if they scattered them. I have no idea what they did.

So, yes, I do write about bereavement quite often, because I know there are many readers who have experienced loss, but don't know how to or don't want to share their feelings. I want young people to see themselves in books in a way that I never did, and, to know that somebody understands. It's important to me.

Paul Canoville

JUST LIKE THAT, I'M BACK DOWN TO EARTH

Paul Canoville is a Black British former professional footballer who played as a winger for Chelsea F.C., and previously for Hillingdon Borough.

For me, to refer to football as "the beautiful game" brings to mind stories of magical lands where everything is possible. For many young people, the idea that nothing is impossible was the dream to hold on to, in order to find ways of escaping or travelling on to greater things. Too often, that dream unravels and you realize that not only does the land of milk and honey not exist, but there is no such thing as the streets being paved with gold. Still, that dream remains for many young people, and thank goodness, because if not then we wouldn't have had Chelsea's first Black football player, Paul Canoville. He graced the football pitch with fantastic displays that helped Chelsea become the team they are today. The pathway that Paul laid for himself and for others can never be disputed, as before 1981, Chelsea had never had a Black member of the team.

He would ask himself why it took so long, and I'm sure if you research the history of Chelsea Football Club, there are some aspects of their past that they're not so proud of. However, there are things that they can be proud of today – for example, Paul now has a suite in his honour at Stamford Bridge, Chelsea's stadium. There is so much admiration for the work Paul has done around race and inclusion, not only for Chelsea and football, but for his community.

Paul's story

Always Black, sometimes blue.

During my career on the pitch, I was used to being in the spotlight, but actually my story is pretty dark at times.

I was born in 1962 in a place called Southall in West London, which, for me, despite its difficulties, actually was the setting for a great childhood. It was tough at times, of course, especially because my sister and I were brought up alone by my mother, who was quite strict, but our little home was full of love, always love. I had to grow up quick and be the man of the house, which wasn't easy at times.

I always wanted to be a footballer.

It was my dream from before I can remember, really – ever since seeing players like Cyrille Regis shine as a Black man on the biggest stage.

My mum was one of the first people to come to the so-called Mother Country on the Windrush. She was told that the streets of Britain were paved with gold – it was a land of money and opportunity. So, despite being young, not even officially a woman yet, she came all the way from Saint Martin on her own when she was just sixteen, to try and get a better life and help Britain recover from the devastation of the Second World War.

My dad came to the UK from Dominica – how my mum and dad met I don't know. Mum wanted to be a nurse, but had to wait until she was eighteen, so in the meantime she stayed at my aunt's and looked for work. She used to always tell me stories of how difficult it was at that time in the late fifties and early sixties, how hard it was for a Black woman – a Black girl, really – because of the colour of her skin.

But she was stubborn and

determined, and I suppose that's where I got it from.

Like most Caribbean mums, my mum believed in discipline, which is exactly what I needed growing up, to be honest. Probably, thinking back to how I was a misunderstood teenager sometimes, I should have grown up in the Caribbean. I wouldn't have dared to mess about back home!

I'm not saying that I don't love England, but I could see the discipline that was needed in me and I know sometimes that my behaviour made it hard for my mum. It's something you don't realize until you grow up. I wasn't rude, I wasn't the naughtiest boy – no way, don't get me wrong. Mum always taught me and June, my sister, to be polite: "Good morning, sir" or "Good morning, miss".

You didn't want to get on the wrong side of Mum. She had this look if I'd done something wrong – without her even saying anything, I'd know about it. It's a skill I mastered myself when I was bringing up my kids and my grandkids, the power of the "non-verbals". That piercing stare, that disapproving glare. I don't have to raise my hand, it's all about the look.

When I grew up, I needed discipline, because in my heart of hearts, I found it difficult after my dad left when I was one or two. It was down to Mum to bring up two kids on her own. And what made it harder was that money was tight, and sometimes I couldn't have the things that some of the other kids had, like new trainers. My mum simply didn't have the money.

In Southall, it was a difficult time to be a young Black boy. Every day there were ongoing battles with racists, like the National Front and skinheads, who wanted to see me kicked out of the country – or worse, dead – just for the colour of my skin. I can't deny, it was really frightening at times. The skinheads used to go around in packs like vultures, attacking Black boys in the streets, going in for the kill, just like that.

THE SCARY THING IS THE POLICE WEREN'T DOING MUCH ABOUT IT.

They never offered us protection – and any time something bad happened to us, they'd say they never found any evidence. When it came down to it, we were on our own. Some days I would be walking with my sister and a car would pass us then slow down. You see the brake lights and you stop because you know what that means, and then you see the car backing up and two white kids coming out of it.

Now I've got to go the long way home, because I'm with my sister. If I'm on my own, I'm facing up to that, but when I'm with my sister, I'm protecting her, and I remember talking and walking all the way, the long way, just to get my sister home safe. My mum would say, "You weren't here on time," and that was a scary thing too. As a Black boy, you'd be walking home from the youth club, down King Street – walking straight home – and the police would just stop you:

"Where are you coming from?" "Youth club." "Where's that?" "Down there."

And they would search you.

"Well, who were you with?

Who do you think you are?

Who do you think you are?"

Next thing, you're in the van, being taken to the station. Now, remember, at this time I'm just a young kid. I was so upset with the police, I was filled with aggression and the need for revenge. That was a difficult time for me. But that's how it was as a young Black boy. If it wasn't the skinheads, it was the police, who would regularly stop me and chuck me in a police cell for no reason.

When I was fifteen, I got caught for a burglary, a first-time offence, and I was sent to borstal (a youth detention centre). That was a wake-up call. Borstal was hard, full of obstacles and challenges to overcome. If you were on your own, you'd get picked on – and you can forget what I said about "overcoming"; that stuff came later.

Sometimes my mouth is too fast.

I don't accept nonsense easily. I used to get angry and upset with how Black people were treated so badly – like, why should we be accepting this now? But borstal changed me, because my freedom was taken away.

I said to the manager of football team I had played with,

"GET ME OUT OF HERE, PLEASE. I BEG YOU, I'LL DO ANYTHING, JUST GET ME OUT OF HERE."

I was in borstal for four months. Alright, I got to meet some guys in there, but what helped me, once again, was my football.

It's funny, I went to borstal on a Friday, joined the football team and played a match on the Sunday. They played an outside team that used to come in, because we weren't allowed out. We played them and won 11–0. I scored nine goals, man, and people were telling me, "You're really good, why don't you go and play for Chelsea?" I went, "Chelsea who?"

I know my time locked up gave my mum heartache.

AS A YOUNG PLAYER JUST STARTING OUT, I DOUBTED MYSELF A LOT. I JUST DIDN'T BELIEVE IN MYSELF.

Everybody kept telling me I was good enough, but I didn't always listen, didn't always believe. My dad never came and to see me play, really. Wasn't there to tell me that I was actually pretty good. My mum never saw me play. Wherever I went when I played football, everybody else had their parents around. Even though my parents weren't there, some of the other parents would say, "Good game. Well done, son. Great game." And all I'm thinking is, *I wish my mum was here to see how good I am*, and my dad too. Instead, when I got home from another Man of the Match performance, my mum would just say, "Paul, you have your chores to do."

Just like that, I'm back down to Earth,

sweeping up the front room. I've just been given Man of the Match! "Mum, I want to talk to you about my goals!" "No, you have dishes to do!" The Caribbean attitude is that you work, you get a professional job. A professional job to them would be a doctor or a policeman. I've already told you about me and the police, and anyway, sometimes my attitude to school wasn't serious enough to fully take in my education.

After coming out of that borstal I started taking football seriously, perhaps even a little too seriously. I joined Hillingdon Borough and then went on trials for bigger clubs – trials at West Bromwich Albion, trials at Southampton. I went to Wimbledon and Tottenham, and then Chelsea. I was scared the first time, to tell you the truth. I knew I was good but I didn't want to make any mistakes. I never gave in. I played for my local club Hillingdon Borough, and I had Winfield boots, Woolworths' own brand, that cost £15. My mother bought them: "You best look after them, because if you don't clean them you isn't playing football no more!"

The next thing you know, the manager is saying to me:

"Paul, you're not playing in the youth team no more."
"What do you mean?"
"You're in the first team!"

I'm sixteen. I'm playing with players that are almost retiring from the game, and I'm the young boy in the first team.

It was going well on the pitch but it was a different story off it...

I had been expelled from school at the age of fifteen.

I bunked off for three terms. When I was supposed to be having mock exams, they told Mum, "It doesn't make sense him taking any, he hasn't been here often enough." Mum used to wake us up in the morning, give us our porridge and then she'd go to work. As soon as she was gone, I'd go back to bed. I'd get to school at noon, in time for school dinner.

It was a whirlwind journey into professional football, another twist in the road, another curve to negotiate: from Southall, trying to avoid swearing skinheads from the National Front, to joining a huge club like Chelsea, not knowing their history, getting through the reserves and making my debut for the first team within four months at the age of twenty.

It was the late John Neal, bless his soul, who gave me my chance in the Chelsea first team. One match day, he came up to me: "You're a substitute, you're playing at Crystal Palace." I was in the match-day squad! I was quickly making phone calls. "You've got to be there! Call everybody, come on. Things are on, things are on!" I would have loved to have called my mum, but she didn't pay any attention, so instead I'm calling my boys and my cousins who know football, and know how good I am.

My sister was the most supportive to me, the one that kept me grounded but also encouraged me to aim high.

The first day, when I signed for Chelsea – the best thing ever – I phoned my sister first.

She said, "Go on, my brother. Go on. Wicked!"

I phoned my best mate, George: "Go on P, well done!"

Better phone Mum.

"Mum, guess what? I'm a professional footballer."
"So what?"
"Alright, Mum. Thanks, bye."

And she meant well, trust me. She's a different woman now, a loving and warm woman who I respect greatly, but she is a product of her generation.

The thing about my experience of racism is that it was hard to open up about it, difficult to share what I was going through to the people who mattered most to me. I learned how to bottle it up, which wasn't good in the long run, not good for my mental or physical health.

Sometimes it was hard to

tell things to my mum.

Back in my school days, when there was trouble, I used to go and tell Mum, but sometimes she blamed me, thought that I must have started it. It's just the way she was, the way she was brought up. So it was hard for me to open up and tell her what was really happening because she didn't always believe me. In the end, when she watched a documentary I featured in about racism in football, we both cried. The tears poured like waterfalls. She had opened up, and it was emotional because at last she was seeing all that I had been through.

I didn't know the history of Chelsea when I went there.

I thought signing for the mighty Blues was going to the greatest day of my life, and it was at the time. But little did I know that there were tough times to come.

I'm making my debut, seventy-nine minutes or so of the match gone versus Sheffield Wednesday, and the manager is telling us substitutes to go and get warmed up. The score is 0–0. I'm walking down the line and all I hear is the "N" word. "Oi, w**, go home." I was thinking, *Oh, man, you've come too far for this.* Those words hurt, but I carried on warming up, tried to get in the zone.

"Hey, _____, go home. We don't want you here." The actual word they called me is far too inappropriate to write here.

Then bananas were thrown at me. Nothing was done. I said, "Wait, are these stewards doing anything here? Are they stopping these people? What's going on?"

I'm starting to get angry now, the people yelling abuse were so nearby. So I turned around, ready to say, "Hey, talk to my face," but these weren't Sheffield Wednesday fans. The people that were racially abusing me were my own club's fans. I'm thinking, *Hold on, you've got a Chelsea flag, you've got a Chelsea shirt on! I'm playing for Chelsea. Your team!*

All that enthusiasm I had for playing professional football,

all those butterflies that I was experiencing because I wanted to do a good job for the club, suddenly all felt pointless. I didn't even want to go on the pitch, that's how bad it was. The manager said to me, "Come on Canoville, get straight." Well, I got on the pitch, I didn't move, I was in shock. This was professional football? I grew up with the National Front marching around in Southall, I grew up with racism at my front door, skinheads in bovver boots thinking they're hard, but all this nonsense going on, here in professional football? I was shocked; I had not expected that. When the referee blew the final whistle I charged straight into the changing room.

My teammates didn't say a word. After a match – especially after a good performance – the changing room is usually the bubbliest place you can think of, pure jokes and laughter and happiness, but this was the quietest changing room ever, because they had heard exactly what happened. What are you going to ask me? "Are you alright, Paul?" A silly question, of course I wasn't. My manager came over and said, "Paul, I don't know how you're feeling. I can only imagine." But it was our fans, the same ones that are paying our wages. What was I going to do? Do I walk away from my dream of being a professional footballer to go … where? I wasn't going to give in that easily, but boy, did I take a lot for three whole years. Home and away. Home and away, I was constantly taking this abuse.

In 1986, I was kicked out of Chelsea. Deep down, I didn't want to leave. The mighty Manchester United came in for me, but Chelsea wouldn't allow me to go there, so I got sold to Reading. It all took its toll and I fell out of love with football for a bit. I didn't even get to say goodbye properly to my teammates, the people who had become my friends. I always said I could never get depressed but I did. It hit me, but I didn't realize it. I was in denial. I was telling people that I didn't need support, but I really did.

When I got into drugs, I was so in denial, I didn't care.

At times I wanted to just take my life, and sometimes I actually tried. But I made the decision to carry on, and that brings us to where I am now.

My role now involves going into schools, doing assemblies and talking to young students. They weren't even born when I was playing for Chelsea, but they do know about me – some check me out first online. I remember a young boy mentioning Wikipedia, and me saying, "Wiki who?" I knew nothing about it, I had to go home and ask my daughter, "Who's Wikipedia?"

I DO LOVE GOING OUT TO SCHOOLS,

though, I have to say. What could be better for me? Now I can talk about the important things. We've got to try and get rid of the racism that exists in society, and if we don't start with young people, they're never going to learn. I talk to them about anything and everything.

When I was a kid, I wasn't bold or forward enough to put up my hand to answer a question. I was one of those who knew the answer, but wouldn't say, just in case I was wrong. I never put up my hand. But when I hear the questions that come out of these kids today, I'm like ... What's going on? How bold! "Mr Canoville, what made you start taking drugs?" And this is why I've started the Paul Canoville Foundation, to help young people believe in themselves.

Racism in football still exists and has probably become even more visible because of social media. Racism is strong, so we have to be stronger. You've got to give confidence to these young players, show them that they shouldn't have to take this abuse and feel threatened if they come and complain about it. That was the case with me, and look how long ago that was ... it's been forty years since I made my debut.

I'm trying to play my

part, trying to get more involved,

because a lot more needs to be done – a lot more. Youngsters now shouldn't be afraid to make their move. We have to speak out and let the FA know this shouldn't be going on, not now, not by today's standards. This is what we really have to push forward.

I like to stay humble, very humble, about what I've got and what I've been given. But I had to fight hard; nothing was easy for me. The one thing I always wanted was to be respected. My peers had the utmost respect for me, and I for them: they taught me a lot, and they weren't just family members, some were elders for me too. They showed courage not just in football, but with whatever they did in life.

I am glad to be here and still alive, to be honest. I am honoured to stand on a platform and share my knowledge and experience. I've been given an opportunity, I know I have. I've been through some difficult times, trust me, but I'm still here, and this is the reason I'm going to give back. Nothing will stop me – any day, any week, there's always something going on with some project I'm involved in.

That's why it's important to ask for help if you need it. You're not weak if you do that, trust me.

I want to say to people:

I'M HERE WHEN YOU NEED ME.

ABOUT THE

Stuart Lawrence is a motivational speaker and youth engagement specialist. His brother, Stephen Lawrence, was murdered in a racially motivated attack in 1993. The Lawrence family's tireless campaign for justice has led to cultural shifts and changes in attitudes towards racism within British society.

Stuart worked as a teacher for fifteen years. He now works within the education system to equip young people with the mindset to believe and achieve what they want in life, no matter the challenges they might face.

With the Stephen Lawrence Foundation, Stuart helps to promote Stephen Lawrence Day, marked each year on 22 April – the day in 1993 that Stephen died. Stephen Lawrence Day is a celebration of his life and legacy; a moment to reflect, to keep the focus on racial inequality and celebrate efforts to remove it.

AUTHOR

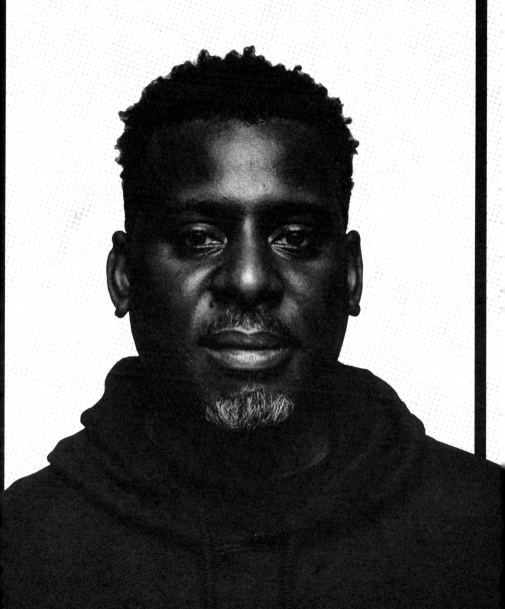

From **role models to self-control**, failure to imagination, Stuart Lawrence talks about what he has learned in life, using his own experience to **help young people harness the good in themselves** and in the world around them, using that **fire of positivity** to create change in their lives.

FIND YOUR VOICE AND BE YOUR BEST SELF

STUART LAWRENCE

SILENCE IS NOT AN OPTION

INSPIRATION

Here's a selection of books and people who have inspired me on my journey through life.

A good book to read:

Long Walk to Freedom by Nelson Mandela – there is an abridged edition available for young readers.

See if any of these authors are on your bookshelves at school:

Julia Donaldson
Dr Seuss
Roald Dahl
Malorie Blackman

For inspiration, check out:

Omari McQueen
Instagram: @omarimcqueen
A young entrepreneur who started his own vegan food business and has his own TV show and cookbook publishing.

Greta Thunberg
Instagram: @gretathunberg
A young campaigner fighting to save our planet in the fight against global warming.

Timothy Armoo
Instagram: @timarmoo
A young entrepreneur who is the Chief Executive Officer of one of the world's leading marketing agencies.

Stormzy
www.stormzy.com
A rapper who rapidly shot to fame and has used his platform to give back to his community through initiatives such as university scholarship funds.

Farzana Khan
Twitter: @khankfarza
A writer and the co-founder and executive director of Healing Justice London, an organization aiming to heal communities and break down barriers.

David Olusoga
Twitter: @DavidOlusoga
A British historian, writer, broadcaster, presenter and filmmaker.

Barack Obama
Instagram: @barackobama
The first Black President of the United States of America, who fought to break down barriers by winning the seat for presidency.

Michelle Obama
Instagram: @michelleobama
Michelle Obama is a lawyer, writer and advocate for women, as well as being the first Black First Lady of the United States.

It would be great to hear what you think of this book. If you have any questions you can contact me at:

@hon_stuartlawrence on Instagram and Tiktok
@sal2nd on Twitter
@hon_stuartlaw on Snapchat

Stay Safe Online

Please remember the golden rules of online life:

- Think about waiting until you're thirteen to use social media.
- Keep your location and personal information private.
- Be smart – don't agree to meet face to face with an online friend, or send them photos of yourself, until you've spoken to an adult you trust.
- Report anything abusive or that makes you feel uncomfortable to a trusted adult.
- Remember your digital footprint – everything you post online is permanent.

ACKNOWLEDGEMENTS

First of all, I'd like to thank all those that have contributed to making this book possible, from Leah James and the whole Scholastic team to all the contributors and the necessary people that helped to pull together this book.

A big shout out to Ashley Hickson-Lovence – thank you, it's been fantastic working with you on this first book, and hopefully many more to come.

Also I'd like to thank you, the reader, because if you don't buy or read the book then it'll just sit on the shelf and you'll never understand these great stories that have contributed to these people's lives.

By reading these stories, it's clear that everyone's journey has a beginning, middle and end, and that their final destination has been reached through hard work, not without ups and downs as well as good and bad days.

Anything is possible, just as long as you believe in the destination you're trying to reach and also making sure you allow others around you to help and support you in getting to that mountaintop.

INDEX

155